Shetland Ponies

by Grace Hansen

Abdo Kids Jumbo is an Imprint of Abdo Kids
abdobooks.com

abdobooks.com

Published by Abdo Kids, a division of ABDO, P.O. Box 398166, Minneapolis, Minnesota 55439.

Abdo Kids Jumbo™ is a trademark and logo of Abdo Kids.

Printed in the United States of America, North Mankato, Minnesota.

052019

092019

Photo Credits: Alamy, iStock, Shutterstock

Production Contributors: Teddy Borth, Jennie Forsberg, Grace Hansen
Design Contributors: Dorothy Toth, Pakou Moua

Library of Congress Control Number: 2018963347

Publisher's Cataloging-in-Publication Data

Names: Hansen, Grace, author.

Title: Shetland ponies / by Grace Hansen.

Description: Minneapolis, Minnesota : Abdo Kids, 2020 | Series: Horses set 2 | Includes online resources and index.

Identifiers: ISBN 9781532185687 (lib. bdg.) | ISBN 9781532186660 (ebook) | ISBN 9781532187155 (Read-to-me ebook)

Subjects: LCSH: Shetland pony--Juvenile literature. | Horses--Juvenile literature.

Classification: DDC 636.16--dc23

Table of Contents

Shetland Ponies

Shetland ponies are native to the **Shetland Islands** of Scotland. They were once used to help the farmers who lived there. They were the perfect size!

Shetlands are called ponies.

But they are adult horses.

These horses may be small.

But they are mighty!

On the Islands, the winters are long. Shetland ponies were **bred** to handle the **harsh** weather.

The pony's **thick** coat keeps it warm. It grows a double coat in the winter months. This protects it from the winds.

A Shetland pony's coat can be any color. The coat can have patches of color. But it should never be spotted like an **Appaloosa's** coat.

Shetland ponies should be

11 **hands** tall or less.

Pros of Being a Pony

On the small islands, there is less grass. This small horse does not need to eat as much as an average-sized horse.

Today, Shetlands can make great riding horses for children.

More Facts

- Shetland ponies have lived in Shetland for more than 2,000 years.
- Shetland ponies were brought over to mainland Britain to help with mining. This was after a law passed in 1847 that said women and children could no longer move coal from the pits.
- This mighty horse can haul twice its weight!

Glossary

Appaloosa - an American horse breed best known for its colorful spotted coat pattern.

bred - made by mating two other horses.

hand - a unit of measurement of a horse's height, equal to 4 inches (10.16 cm).

harsh - rough and not pleasing.

Shetland Islands - a subarctic group of islands that lie northeast of Great Britain and about 170 miles (280 km) from the Scottish mainland.

thick - having parts that are very close to one another; dense.

Index

Visit **abdokids.com** to access crafts, games, videos, and more!

Use Abdo Kids code

HSK5687

or scan this QR code!